KNIVES IN HENS

David Harrower

ABERDEEN COLLEGE
GORDON LIBRARY

WITHDRAWN

Methuen Dram

A Methuen Modern Play

Copyright © 1995, 1997 by David Harrower

The right of David Harrower to be identified as the author of this work has been asserted by him in accordance with the Copyright, Designs and Patents Act, 1988

First published in Great Britain in 1995
This revised version first published in Great Britain in 1997
by Methuen Publishing Ltd
11–12 Buckingham Gate,
London SW1E 6LB

3 5 7 9 10 8 6 4

A CIP catalogue record for this book is available from the British Library

ISBN 10: 0 413 72110 8
ISBN 13: 978 0 413 72110 5

Typeset by Deltatype Ltd, Birkenhead, Merseyside
Printed and bound in Great Britain by Cox & Wyman Ltd,
Reading Berkshire

Caution

TRAVERSE
THEATRE

TRAVERSE THEATRE COMPANY
presents

KNIVES IN HENS

by David Harrower

Gilbert Horn	Liam Brennan
Pony William	Lewis Howden
Young Woman	Pauline Knowles

with music composed and performed by
Allan Henderson

Director	Philip Howard
Designer	Mark Leese
Lighting Designer	Chahine Yavroyan
Voice Coach	Ros Steen
Stage Manager	Gavin Johnston
Deputy Stage Manager	Kay Courteney-Chrystal
Assistant Stage Manager	Victoria Paulo
Wardrobe Supervisor	Lynn Ferguson
Wardrobe Assistant	Alice Taylor

First performed at the Traverse Theatre
Friday 2 June 1995; first performance of this
production Sunday 3 August 1997.

DAVID HARROWER

David Harrower lives in Glasgow. KNIVES IN HENS was his first professionally produced play and has since been produced in London (by the Traverse at the Bush Theatre) and Berlin, and will soon be seen in Scandinavia, Austria and New York. Other work includes: A QUIET NIGHT IN (KtC), the libretto for the opera CAT MAN'S TALE (Opera Circus; to be produced in the autumn of 1997) and an adaptation of John Wyndham's novel THE CHRYSALIDS (Royal National Theatre's *BT National Connections*). A short play written for the Barracke, the studio of the Deutches Theater will be staged as part of the 43rd Berlin Festival in September 1997. David is currently under commission to the Traverse and Royal Court Theatres, and the Royal National Theatre Studio.

TRAVERSE THEATRE

Over the last three decades Edinburgh's Traverse Theatre has had a seminal influence on British and international theatre. With quality, award-winning productions and programming, the Traverse receives accolades at home and abroad from audiences and critics alike.

Traverse productions have been seen world-wide. Most recently, WIDOWS toured the UK and BONDAGERS toured the world, delighting audiences in London, Toronto and Budapest. After sell-out Edinburgh runs MOSCOW STATIONS transferred to both the West End and New York; UNIDENTIFIED HUMAN REMAINS transferred to London's Hampstead Theatre; and after touring the Highlands and Islands of Scotland KNIVES IN HENS transferred to a sell-out season at the Bush Theatre in London. No stranger to awards, the Traverse recently won the *Scotland on Sunday Critics' Award* for SHINING SOULS by Chris Hannan.

As Scotland's new writing theatre, the Traverse is a powerhouse of quality experimentation, artistic diversity and the place to see the most important contemporary theatre work. The Theatre commissions the best new writers from Scotland and around the world; facilitates numerous script development workshops, rehearsed readings and public writing workshops; and aims to produce six major new theatre productions plus a Scottish touring production each year.

An essential element of the Traverse Company's activities takes place within the educational sector, concentrating on the process of new writing in schools. The Traverse is unique in its exclusive dedication to new writing, providing the infrastructure, professional support and expertise to ensure the development of a sustainable and relevant theatre culture for Scotland and the UK.

LIAM BRENNAN (*Gilbert Horn*): For the Traverse: WORMWOOD. Other theatre work includes seasons and productions with the Dundee Rep, Perth Rep, Borderline, Cumbernauld Theatre, Salisbury Playhouse, Castlemilk People's Theatre, The Brunton Theatre, Durham Theatre Company and Calypso Productions, Dublin. Productions include: MONTROSE (Royal Lyceum); MERCHANT OF VENICE (Sheffield Crucible); GOD SAVED IRELAND CRIED THE HERO (Wiseguise, 1996 Edinburgh Festival); BABYCAKES (Clyde Unity). TV includes: TAGGART, STRATHBLAIR II, HIGH ROAD, MACHAIR. Radio includes numerous plays and short stories for BBC Radio Scotland and Radio Clyde.

PHILIP HOWARD (*Director*): Trained: Royal Court Theatre on the Regional Theatre Young Director Scheme. Associate Director of the Traverse, 1993-6, and Artistic Director since September 1996. Productions at the Traverse include: LOOSE ENDS, BROTHERS OF THUNDER, GRACE IN AMERICA, EUROPE, MARISOL, KNIVES IN HENS (also Bush Theatre), THE ARCHITECT, FAITH HEALER and WORMWOOD. For the Royal Court Young People's Theatre: THROWING STONES and the 1991 Young Writers' Festival. Other theatre includes HIPPOLYTUS (Cambridge); ENTERTAINING MR SLOANE (Royal, Northampton); SOMETHING ABOUT US (Lyric Hammersmith Studio). Philip was a director at Dràma Nàiseanta na h-Oigridh on the Isle of Benbecula from its foundation in 1989 until 1992.

LEWIS HOWDEN (*Pony William*): For the Traverse: KNIVES IN HENS (also Bush Theatre), LOOSE ENDS, HOUSE AMONG THE STARS. Other theatre work includes: CUTTIN' A RUG, CHANGED DAYS (Royal Lyceum); THE WITCHES OF POLLOK, THE TRICK IS TO KEEP BREATHING (Tron); QUELQUES FLEURS, TARTUFFE

(Nippy Sweeties); ELECTRA (Diva); GLENGARRY GLEN ROSS, THE CRUCIBLE (Arches); THE BRUCE (Brunton); THE SECRET VOICE (TAG); A NIGHT IN THE SARRY (Unit One). TV and film work includes: TAGGART, DR FINLAY (STV); STRATHBLAIR, THE BLUE BOY; ROSALEEN, CALEDONIANS AND ROMANS (BBC); THE CHIEF (Anglia); TURNING WORLD (Channel 4); GARE AU MALE (Animula). Radio includes: THE BLASPHEMER (BBC).

PAULINE KNOWLES (*Young Woman*): For the Traverse: WIDOWS, THE COLLECTION, MARISOL, KNIVES IN HENS (also Bush Theatre). Other theatre work includes: MEN SHOULD WEEP, A SCOTS QUAIR (TAG); SWING HAMMER SWING (Citizens'); ELEGIES FOR ANGELS, PUNKS AND RAGING QUEENS (Luckenbooth); TWELFTH NIGHT (Royal Lyceum & Salisbury Theatre); CUTTIN' A RUG, SCHOOL FOR WIVES (Royal Lyceum); ANTIGONE, JUMP THE LIFE TO COME (7:84); OH WHAT A LOVELY WAR, SHARKS, CLEANING UP (Wildcat); VODKA AND DAISIES (Annexe); DON JUAN (Penname); ALADDIN (Skint Knees). Television includes: ACTING WITH RICHARD WILSON, STRATHBLAIR, JOHN BROWN'S BODY. Radio includes: FLOATING, SUBUTU PASSAGE, WANTIN' A HAND, LEAVE ME ALONE.

MARK LEESE (*Designer*): For the Traverse: ANNA WEISS, WIDOWS, FAITH HEALER, THE HOPE SLIDE, BROTHERS OF THUNDER, KNIVES IN HENS (also Bush Theatre). Other theatre work includes: PARALLEL LINES (Theatre Cryptic); FROGS (Royal National Theatre); BRILLIANT TRACES (Diva/Tron); BABES IN THE WOOD, SNOW WHITE, LOVE & LIBERTY (Tron); BORN GUILTY, THE WAR IN HEAVEN, THE GRAPES OF WRATH, THE SALT WOUND, ANTIGONE (7:84); ON GOLDEN POND (Royal Lyceum); BLACK COMEDY, PUBLIC EYE (Watford Palace). Film includes: CALIFORNIA SUNSHINE (Sigma Films); GOOD DAY FOR THE BAD GUYS (Greenbridge Films); WHAT ELEPHANTS (WWF).

CHAHINE YAVROYAN (*Lighting Designer*): Trained: Bristol Old Vic School. For the Traverse: THE ARCHITECT, SHINING SOULS. Other theatre work includes: THE TRIAL, METAMORPHOSIS, MISS JULIE, ZOO STORY, AGAMEMNON (Stephen Berkoff); PEOPLE SHOWS NO.84 to NO.101... and counting; MACBETH (Leicester Haymarket); USES OF ENCHANTMENT (ICA); THE LITTLE BLACK BOOK (French Institute); ENNIO MARCHETTO (Hackney Empire); LA MUSICA DEUXIEME, GAUCHO (Hampstead); HEDDA GABLER, WOLK'S WORLD (Manchester Royal Exchange); PYGMALION (Nottingham Playhouse); DARWIN'S FLOOD (Bush); TANTAMOUNT ESPERANCE (Royal Court); HAMLET (Kaboodle). Dance work includes: 15 MINUTES TO 6 HOURS (Anatomy Dance Theatre); GLORIA, I SURRENDER DEAR (The Place); HAUGHMOND DANCES (Haughmond Abbey); ASCENDING FIELDS (Fort Dunlop); FOREST DANCES (Purcell Room). Site specific work includes: HOUSE (Station House Opera, Salisbury) and various events and celebrations for the city of Bologna, Italy.

**KNIVES IN HENS props, costumes & scenery
built by Traverse workshops.**
Funded by the National Lottery

**For generous help with KNIVES IN HENS
the Traverse Theatre thanks:**
Macro, Chancelot Mill, Woodhall Mill, Royal Lyceum Theatre Company, James Lindsay & Sons Plc, Edinburgh Fruitmarket. LEVER BROTHERS for Wardrobe Care.
Print Photography by Euan Myles.
Production Photography by Kevin Low.

TRAVERSE THEATRE • SPONSORSHIP

Sponsorship income enables the Traverse to commission and produce new plays and offer audiences a diverse and exciting programme of events throughout the year.

We would like to thank the following companies for their support throughout the year.

CORPORATE ASSOCIATE SCHEME

LEVEL ONE
Dundas & Wilson CS
Scottish Brewers
Scottish Life Assurance Co
United Distillers

LEVEL TWO
Allingham & Co, Solicitors
Isle of Skye 8 Year Blend
Laurence Smith - Wine Merchants
NB Information
Mactaggart and Mickel Ltd
Métier Recruitment
Willis Corroon Scotland Ltd

LEVEL THREE
Alistir Tait FGA Antique & Fine Jewellery, Gerrard & Medd, Designers,
KPMG, Moores Rowland Chartered Accountants,
Nicholas Groves Raines Architects,
Scottish Post Office Board

With thanks to:
Navy Blue Design, designers for the Traverse
and to George Stewarts the printers.
Robin Arnott of the Royal Bank of Scotland for his advise on information technology and systems.
This placement was arranged through Business In The Arts.

The Traverse Theatre's work would not be possible without the support of:

 •EDINBVRGH•
THE CITY OF EDINBURGH COUNCIL

The Traverse receives financial assistance for its educational and development work from:
Calouste Gulbenkian Foundation,
Esmee Fairbairn Charitable Trust,
The Peggy Ramsay Foundation,
The Nancie Massey Charitable Trust
Scottish International Education Trust
Charity No.SC 002368

TRAVERSE THEATRE • THE COMPANY

Knives in Hens

for George Gunn

'I care for nobody, no not I, if nobody care for me.'

Knives in Hens was commissioned by and first performed at the Traverse Theatre, Edinburgh, on 2 June 1995 and transferred to the Bush Theatre, London, on 28 November 1995. The cast was as follows:

Young Woman	Pauline Knowles
Pony William	Lewis Howden
Gilbert Horn	Michael Nardone

Directed by Philip Howard
Designed by Mark Leese
Music composed and performed by Martyn Bennett

Characters

Young Woman, *a field-hand*
Pony William, *a ploughman*
Gilbert Horn, *a miller*

Scene One

Rural place.

Cottage at the end of a village. Evening.

Young Woman I'm not a field. How'm I a field? What's a field? Flat. Wet. Black with rain. I'm no field.

William Never said that.

Young Woman Says I'm a field sitting here.

William Said you're like a field.

Young Woman Said I'm a field sitting here.

William Said you're like a field. Like a field.

Young Woman 'S the same.

William Nothing close, woman.

Young Woman If I'm like a field must be a field.

William (*laughs*) Don't have to be a thing to be like it.

Young Woman How?

William Just don't.

Young Woman 'M I other things? Fire?

William I got mud for feet. Can't feel them.

Young Woman ... Shoe? Bed? Door?

William 'S what it's for ... Like.

Young Woman Never heard it 'fore.

William Like, woman. The moon's like cheese. 'S like cheese. But it's not.

Young Woman You been up there? The moon's the moon. Why's it like cheese?

William Always been said. (*Hears something.*) What's that? The horses?

Young Woman So's cheese like the moon?

William Nnh. I'll go in and see them. They're not right.

Young Woman 'S cheese like the moon?

William I know more'n you.

Young Woman Know that.

William You're like any thing I want. I say you were like a field. You were like it, sitting there. Not now. 'S gone. You're not like this field sitting there now.

Young Woman Tell you what I'm like. I'm like nothing but me.

William You got a good shape.

Young Woman You got a good shape.

William Good shape now. Best in the village.

Young Woman 'S that field? (*He feels her.*) You tell me. 'S that field?

William You haven't seen the field.

Young Woman This's one field?

William Not many in the village know it.

Young Woman Where's it?

William Out-bye.

Young Woman I work on fields all over.

William Walk that way.

Young Woman Have before now.

William 'S the furthest over. The last field.

Young Woman I seen every field there is.

William 'S a good field. Good size. In all my years I've never seen it cheat or be stubborn or hold a grudge like others. Was made for a man, a horse and a plough. 'S flat and good 'til its end when it slopes but nothing that tires

you. The soil's good and rich – so crops grow out the
same. When it's rested the grass that grows's good too,
and's the sweetest anywhere round here. Horses'll tell you
that after grazing. See now, woman.

Young Woman I'll walk to it one day. Walk back and
tell you what I seen.

William I need washing 'fore I go to the horses.

Young Woman (*as she leaves*) Cheese the other women
make's like the moon. My cheese's like cheese.

William Before, I lay there and the horses'd be grazing
slowly around me. Once I looked up and all that's my
body'd gone inside out. All that's me on a circle of out-bye
grass. Red. Wet. Rabbit hearts tied up with cow's saliva.
I've never said a thing. Clouds came off me same's when
I've pulled a new horse out in December. Nearly gone
now, that. 'Fore it got dark I led them back, down the
village to the stables, with this field still in my head. Why'd
it come to me? Was only a boy. Could've lived in that field
all my life if they let me. Mud's stinking.

Scene Two

Open ground.

Young Woman *enters carrying a basket.*

Young Woman The wind blows. The sun shines. The
crops grow. The sky – ... The bird – flies. The clouds –
... The tree ... What? Stands. The tree stands. The sky –
... The sky – ... The rabbit runs. The clouds – ... run?
... grow? The leaves on the tree – ... hang? The sky –
... The sky – ...

Scene Three

Fields.

William *in shirtsleeves, eating.* **Young Woman** *sits. Between them the uncovered basket.*

William   You ill?

Young Woman   No.

William   Fever?

Young Woman   No.

William   What? Something wrong with you.

Young Woman   Nothing.

William   Seen you.

Young Woman   Walking to here. With food for you and the plough-horse.

William   Seen you standing there. What you doing?

Young Woman   I was looking. I was looking at . . .

William   What . . . ?

Young Woman   I saw a . . . a puddle, a puddle you can see the earth under. Clear water puddle after fresh rain. See the cracks in the earth there. See birdsfeet. See the sun shining. You got a name for that?

William   Puddle.

Young Woman   No. The right name.

William   Right name's puddle.

Young Woman   How?

William   You go straight to places, woman. You walk and don't stand.

Young Woman   Puddle's dark, mud water. See nothing in it. What was that I saw? Clear shining water. What?

William   Puddle. Still puddle. I've said 'fore. Dark puddle, clear puddle. 'S the same.

Young Woman   Things change each time I look at them.

William   Some do. Some don't. Keep with what you know. Best way. No standing looking. Village'll see. And talk. You know this village.

Young Woman   I don't know much. Don't know enough. When the wind makes the tree do this . . . (*Shakes herself.*) What's that? There a name for that? Why's it do it? See straight under the leaves then. Dunno'f it's right to look. What's that?

William   You'll get them. You'll get to know. You doubt God?

Young Woman   No. Never doubt God.

William   You're young still, 's why. I'm not. You'll get to know. Hear me? No more of it. What you done this morning?

Young Woman   After you left, I killed two hens and fed the rest. I gave one away for a bag of salt; the other I hung over the fire to dry. I pulled four carrots from the earth and washed them. I drew fresh water from the well. I poured a candle with the last of the tallow. I dropped a knife on the cottage floor. I tanned a hide. I boiled stones in butter and kept the sauce. I weaved a blanket for our winter beds. I combed my hair for lice. I dropped to my knees and prayed. I stared at my hands. I brought food to you and the horse.

He eats, raises brow at the dropped knife, looks to the horse.

William   We've worked each other hard since sun-up. You not eating?

Young Woman   I'll watch you. 'S better. Eat's a horse.

He imitates a masticating horse – uncannily. She laughs.

William   'S one thing you'll find every one has in

common. Every one likes to eat. Never met man or woman who hasn't. Even them in other parts, they like it.

Young Woman   'S that what's in your head when you plough? 'S that what you see? Other places. Other people. Eating.

William   All ploughmen get tired of looking down at the earth. Black. Hurts the back and neck. Looked left or right they'd fall. I look up at the sky. But it hurts my neck and eyes.

Young Woman   We're not to look up there long. Our faces'd be on top of our heads, flat, if we were.

William   Know that.

Young Woman   God watches every thing. He sees every thing. He has the names for every thing.

William   'S right. Our faces are here, north side, to look straight ahead.

Young Woman   There's all we need to look at between our earth and his sky. I'm glad's us.

William   Glad's us what?

Young Woman   Glad's us got married. If I hadn't married you I'd have married someone else but it wouldn't be the same. Said that soon's I seen you.

William   Pour me some milk.

Young Woman   Like kissing your cock.

William   Here. Eat.

Scene Four

Outside cottage.

Very early morning. **Young Woman** *calling, walks to the stable.*

Young Woman   William? William?

William Ssh. Ssh. There. All right now. Quiet.

Young Woman William, William, will-he-be-here?
William, William, will-he-be-there? (*Enters.*) William!

William SHUT YOUR MOUTH WOMAN OR BY
GOD HIMSELF I'LL DO IT FOR YOU!!!! Woman? . . .
'S what I said day we married. You don't come in the
stable without asking me. Puts the fear in the horses. They
dunno what't is. Scares them.

Young Woman Sorry, William . . . How long till I can?

William Don't speak for horses. Could be another
summer. They got to trust your smell. And your voice.
Each of them.

Young Woman . . . Where're you?

William Stall on the end.

Young Woman The bed was empty. And cold.

William I was out most'f the night.

Young Woman (*moving further in*) What's . . . ?

William Stay back! This mare, she's in trouble. She's
shaking.

Young Woman She dying?

William No. She got a young one inside her.

Young Woman That it?

William 'S her first time, woman.

Young Woman You be's quick when I'm carrying our
first.

William Go in, woman. 'S cold.

Young Woman Know which one it was?

William Him there. Told him to stay away. (*To horse.*)
You know that's what I said. Stay away. Last time I trust
that one. Now go in.

Young Woman You coming in?

William Told you. She needs me here.

Young Woman Not having it now's she?

William No. But I'm not leaving her. She dunno where she is. She's only a girl.

Young Woman Horses you want to be with, not me. Live in this stable.

William This's me, woman. You know that.

Young Woman There's boys in the village'd help you.

William Don't want 'em. These horses are special. Boys aren't. 'S you I want with me. And you'll do it. Now go'n eat. 'S you doing my work today.

Young Woman What's wanting done?

William Must know that. Grain. 'S needing ground.

Young Woman I've to go to the mill?

William I'm staying with her.

Young Woman Want me going out there?

William 'S what I said.

Young Woman . . . Today?

William You want it all to rot and us starve? Hh? The cart's loaded. 'N take bastard there. (*Horse.*) Away from me.

Young Woman They say's him killed his wife and the child she was giving birth to. 'N there's disappeared men and women who're cats and goats and monkeys now. Go from market to market, sleeping together and singing for food.

William He knows you've me. Knows what I'd do.

Young Woman Since I was a girl they've talked of the miller.

William All you need's hate for him. 'S what he expects.

Every bone of your body. Hate. 'S a village custom.

Young Woman   I do hate him!

William   Again.

Young Woman   I HATE him!

William   Stronger!

Young Woman   I HATE HIM!! Show him you're afraid, 's how it starts. I hate every miller there is. Throw them in a pond and watch their bodies swell and stink.

William   You got it now. Eleventh of a peck, he gets. He can't steal more. You tell him – pull them sleeves up, miller.

Young Woman   Pull them sleeves up, miller!

William   . . . when he weighs the flour. Eleventh of a peck. Bastard. 'N you watch him. You watch our grain.

Scene Five

Mill.

Soft sound of a river.

Young Woman *unloads the first grain-sack with much effort.*
Gilbert Horn *appears, watches her. She becomes aware but carries on.*

Gilbert   You wanting help with your sacks?

Young Woman (*low*)   You stay away from me, boy.

Gilbert   Said d'you want help with your grain.

Young Woman   No. Don't need your help.

Gilbert   Makes it –

Young Woman   I do it alone!

Gilbert   First time for you here.

Young Woman   I know what gets done.

Gilbert   Know it's long, empty work then. Where's the husband? Lying ill and useless in bed?

Young Woman   He's in the fields, pushing a plough, fit and strong.

Gilbert   Knows his wife's a fair strength herself. Sending her alone.

Young Woman   I wasn't sent, miller-man. I came. Now get the stone turning. I want finished quick.

Gilbert   Come and tell it yourself. 'S beautiful, no? You want finished quick? Tell it. Stone turns only for itself. Listens to no one. Not even a woman on her own. You'll sit and wait like all the others. Husband not tell you that?

Young Woman   Where's the grain go?

Gilbert   There. I'll open the river for the wheel. Go into my house. There's fire and a stool to sit on.

Young Woman   I'm standing here.

Gilbert   The stone's old. Takes time.

Young Woman   Right here, I said.

Gilbert   When it turns you want no ears.

Young Woman   Standing here till I see my flour.

He goes. Wheel starts to turn. The noise grows, becomes deafening. She endures it, shaking, hands to her ears. Finally runs out.

Scene Six

Gilbert's *house.*

He sits at a table. **Young Woman** *comes to the door.*

Young Woman   Freezing in there.

Gilbert   You want some ale. A dram? (*Shakes her head.*) Coming in or staying there?

Young Woman   Stand right where I am.

Gilbert   You won't care if I take a drop?

Young Woman   Don't care any thing you do. 'S your house.

He drinks, then yawn-shouts.

Gilbert   Aaauuhhhh. Oh . . . work . . . work . . . work . . .

Young Woman   Must break your back that stone doing the work.

Gilbert   Ih?

Silence. He drinks more.

Takes special men to be millers. Men who work hard. Alone. In ways villages know nothing of.

Long silence. Finally points to the door.

See that? There. There. 'S a name. You know it? Door-stump. That's my door-stump . . . 'S that not what your village believes?

Young Woman   What?

Gilbert   When a thing's got a name 's got a use?

Young Woman   Dunno what you're . . . Not getting me to shut this door, miller-man.

Gilbert   Stop that cold air freezing up 'my house'.

Young Woman   I want to see my grain.

Gilbert   'S staying there.

Young Woman   I came with five sacks . . .

Gilbert   Well counted.

Young Woman   I'm leaving with five sacks.

Gilbert   How'd I get it sat here?

He gets up for more drink. Begins to whistle softly. She's getting more frantic, watching her grain, watching him.

Young Woman   You stop! Stop!

Gilbert   Ih?

Young Woman   Get my husband out to you, boy! Said stop! . . . Why you laughing? STOP!!

Gilbert   They got another living in the ground. Dirt in your eyes, field-hand. Mouth flapping in the wind. Ears open. Shovels filled them with the names of Gilbert Horn. What you got rotting in there?

Young Woman   I got nothing there.

Gilbert   No? Not the power of magic I have? The death charms? Not which plants're to be picked special. Not which bones and eyes of animals and birds need kept and powdered? Nothing of my wife and child? Not that I killed them both? Not that I've no want of family? None've that in there?

Young Woman   Evil-breath!

Begins to inch out backwards.

Gilbert   Where you going, dung-brain?

Young Woman   Away from your evil, bastard.

Gilbert   That village's death. Nothing.

Young Woman   Not taking my eyes off you, boy. Not turning my back. You'll die you touch me.

He turns away, sits down again. She's almost out.

Gilbert   . . . 'S you married that Pony William, wasn't it?

She freezes.

'S who shares your bed. The village ploughman. Pony William . . .

Young Woman   No. No.

Gilbert   No?

Young Woman   You leave him.

Gilbert   That not his name? Pony William.

Young Woman   'S name's William.

Gilbert   I hear Pony William.

Young Woman   You don't say that.

Gilbert   'S what most in the village call him.

Young Woman   Liar.

Gilbert   I hear them. Pony William –

Young Woman   Liar!

Gilbert   'N Pony's bride.

Young Woman   I'd spit on them say that.

Gilbert   Heard's 'cos of his love for the younger horses.

Young Woman   No . . .

Gilbert   No? . . . Just the one horse? Special horse?

Young Woman   . . . That's envy.

Gilbert   Envy? Not heard that spoke in a long time. 'S
the village tell you what it is?

Young Woman   'Course.

Gilbert   How's that envy?

Young Woman   Envy of us back there. In the village.

Gilbert   Envy of you and Pony and them others all living
in a death place? All them rotted lives? How've I envy?

Young Woman   I know. 'S a look. The eyes. Like evil.

Gilbert   Do it.

Young Woman   What?

Gilbert   Envy.

Young Woman   Can't.

Gilbert   Why?

Young Woman   Haven't got it. Stupid.

Gilbert   'S what they say.

Young Woman   Who?

Gilbert   'S that what you seen?

Young Woman   What?

Gilbert   Horses come first with him.

Young Woman   No. Loves me first.

Gilbert   First.

Young Woman   'N always.

Gilbert   Then you won't like it?

Young Woman   I like love. Better'n evil.

Gilbert   You don't like them calling him Pony William?

Young Woman   You leave that name I said.

Gilbert   You don't like Pony William.

Young Woman   NO. No.

Gilbert   Then there you are.

Young Woman   Where?

Gilbert   What power've you over others' tongues?

She leaves.

Scene Seven

Cottage.

William *comes on to find* **Young Woman** *there.*

William   You left our sacks there, woman?

Young Woman   That miller's stone's old and weak.
Stood freezing as he sat.

William   All my grain left with that miller –

Young Woman   Still our grain tomorrow, William.

William   'N how do I sleep tonight.

Young Woman   We'll sleep. Then you take the horse
and cart tomorrow. Flour'll be ground then. Ready.

William   You wanting me to go back?

Young Woman   I'll stay with the mare. Or go to the
fields.

William   Back 'n find him sitting there laughing.

Young Woman   No. He knows you. Knows what you'd
do.

William   No? Not laughing? The miller who does
nothing. Sitting there with our five sacks at his feet. Who
never walks a field or pushes a plough. Pushing his hands
into the grain we grew. We've given him all he wants. The
miller who's afraid of the land. Not laugh, woman? You go
into his house?

Young Woman   Stood freezing as he sat.

William   Place he never leaves. Where he sits and talks.

Young Woman   'N talks and talks.

William   'S what he'll do to the next goes to his mill.
Tell them of the ploughman and his wife who ran when
she was afraid.

Young Woman   I didn't run.

William   The wife who left the grain behind. Be him, the
bastard miller, talking 'bout us then. Can't be me goes
back, woman. You had good hate of him. Where's it gone?
Only fear now. Where's the hate?

Young Woman   I had it. Going there. But's him. Close
by. Looking.

William 'Cos he sees what he'll never have.

Young Woman What?

William Good strong wife. Know that, woman. Don't have to say it. Had my eye on you for years. Watched you grow. Picked you to be my wife. Who'd work same's me. Who'd sweat same's me. Who'd only listen to what's right. Listen to the stone, not the miller. All he's got's that mouth. To talk all day and all night to no one. 'S nothing. Now go back. Go. Be my wife.

Scene Eight

Countryside.

Young Woman The sun warms the wind that blows. The wind pushes the clouds under the sky. Black cloud holds the rain. White cloud ... The bird flies under the white cloud – into the tree. Tree's for wood. The bird's for ... One bird. One's lucky, two's unlucky, three's health, four's wealth, five's sickness, and six is death. Dead bird, bake a pie. The wind pushes the white cloud under the sun. White cloud's for ... The rabbit runs on the field. Rabbit's food. The bird – the tree ... loses the bird. Bird's gone. The wind pushes the white cloud off the sun. White cloud's for ... White cloud's for ...

Scene Nine

Gilbert's *house.*

Gilbert *sits at his table, writing on paper with an ink pen.*
Young Woman *appears, remains in the doorway. She watches him and also the pen. Finally he looks up, across at her.*

Gilbert Still five. You counted? Still five there, ih?

Pause.

Last sack's on.

Young Woman   I seen that.

Gilbert   Where'd you go?

Young Woman   Had other work to do. Couldn't stand wasting time. Hearing talk about nothing.

Gilbert   Won't be long to stand now.

A long pause.

Young Woman   'S a new stone you need, miller. I'm wanting to get home 'fore the sky goes black.

Gilbert   Stonemason's nearly finished the new one. When he's done your village men'll roll it out here, to me.

He writes again.

Young Woman   . . . What you got there?

Gilbert   What?

Young Woman   . . . that.

Gilbert   This? You don't know what this is? 'S a pen. Ink pen.

Young Woman   What you wanting with that?

Gilbert   Sold to me at market by a travelling musician.

Young Woman   Food-money spent on a useless stick.

Gilbert   'S worth the price.

Young Woman   Flour you steal from us 's what bought it.

Gilbert   See how the firelight shines on it.

Young Woman   What's it – feed you?

Gilbert   No.

Young Woman   Warm you?

Gilbert   'S a good weight in the hand.

Young Woman Waste.

Gilbert Write with it too.

Young Woman What?

Gilbert I . . . write . . .

Young Woman What d'you write?

Gilbert What I've done.

Young Woman Grind corn. Stop grinding corn. Grind corn. Stop grinding corn.

Gilbert More'n that.

Young Woman Must be the laird's new game. Only he'd write down the nothing he does. You wanting to be the laird now, miller?

Gilbert I've more life than corn. I write what's in here, in my head. End of the day, every day. Here . . . to here.

Holds up a sheaf of papers.

Look how much of me there is. Can tell what's in my head yesterday, or . . . last winter, and most days since.

Young Woman Then's an evil trick!

Gilbert Evil?

Young Woman Ready for the fire.

Gilbert Evil – this? How?

Young Woman 'S God puts things in your head and's him who takes them away. 'S sin to keep them.

Gilbert Field-hand, could not be God gave us this . . .

Young Woman Not us.

Gilbert . . . so's we can know more'f the world?

Young Woman 'S an evil stick you made.

Gilbert I can tell who's come to my mill, who's stood outside, who's come in to drink, who's said not a word,

who's cursed me over and over, who's stood in my
doorway, who's been so afraid of Gilbert Horn they turned
and ran back to the village with their husband's ... (*Writes.*)
... horse and cart.

Pause. She realises.

Young Woman   You take that off there!

Gilbert   Ink's dry now.

Young Woman   ... Then burn it. Do it, bastard! Give it
to the fire.

Gilbert   I thank him I wasn't born in that village. 'S a
black pit. Pulled from the womb older'n when you die.
Elders stand at the bed-end and use knives to drain away
the blood. Dark night's what's left round your bones. Pull
out eyes and leave cold pebbles in the hollows.

Young Woman   You reek of evil filth words, boy!

Gilbert   Evil – what else's a villager say faced with a
man got eyes and tongue who're trusted friends? Man who
looks slow and close at the world for all the names it's got.
'Sky's going black?' Not over me. I live under different sky.

Young Woman   'S earth we'll put you under – fill you
over. Stop up that mouth.

Gilbert   I'll be you then. Under earth. Seeing nothing out
pebble eyes. Seeing nothing.

Young Woman   I see.

Gilbert   Knowing nothing.

Young Woman   I see. Know what I see.

Gilbert   Track. Mud. Horse. Here. There. Sky ...

Young Woman   See more'n that. I got names for most
things in God's world.

Gilbert   Tell me what.

Young Woman   I'll tell you nothing. Not giving you
what's in my head.

Gilbert   Stink of shit, 's why.

Young Woman   I got things ... I got things. Not speaking them.

Gilbert *leans over, places the pen on side of table nearest to her.*

Gilbert   Then write them.

Young Woman   Not touching that ...

Gilbert   Write what you seen coming to my mill. Show me the village 's more'n peasants with rotting shit in their heads.

Young Woman   Stone you for that.

Gilbert   'Course ...

Young Woman   You wanting stoned? I'll tell them.

Gilbert   Can't write.

Young Woman   I can write, boy!

Gilbert   Prove it. (*Shakes her head.*) How's this evil? You write.

Young Woman   'S chalk we had.

Gilbert   Pen's better chalk.

Young Woman   Still not getting any thing from my head.

Gilbert   What'll I do? Only ink on paper.

Young Woman   Dunno. Some thing.

Gilbert   After you write I'll put it in the fire.

Young Woman   'S tricks.

Gilbert   Then you take it. Carry it home. Show Pony what you can do.

Young Woman *hesitates.*

Young Woman   No ... Why d'you want what's in here? 'S mine.

Gilbert   How'll anyone ever know? (*Silence.*) You can write, ih?

Young Woman   Said I could.

Gilbert   Then give me something outside you. That all the village knows.

Young Woman   What you wanting, miller?

Gilbert   ... Your name.

Silence. Finally she comes to the table. He pushes paper towards her.

Young Woman   No tricks.

Gilbert   None.

She has difficulty mastering the pen. Resolute.

Young Woman   Show you I'm no dung-brain.

She holds the paper up so he can read.

Gilbert   Tell you what, horse-wife. You're beautifully named.

They look at each other. He gets up. She moves back to the door with the paper.

Your flour's ready. I got to take what's mine.

Scene Ten

Cottage.

William   Here's wife. She've any more trouble with Killer-miller? (*Shakes her head.*) She stable the horse right? (*Nod.*) She come back with our five sacks? (*Nod.*) She keep a close eye on the flour? (*Nod.*) She wanting a bowl of meal?

(*Shake.*) She'll find them husks get everywhere. She'll feel they're growing under her skin. She'll find water to wash with. She'll be thankful for her husband's hand.

She goes to the water. Wearily looks down at herself, gives a small scream when she sees the black marks that are on the thumb and forefinger of one hand.

Young Woman   Auh. . . !

William   . . . What's it, woman?

Young Woman *freezes.*

Young Woman   Spark. From the fire. William, we can go straight to bed.

William   No washing?

Young Woman   Could you not take sweat and roughness on you for a night?

William*'s eyes widen, grins.*

William   No better words spoke since we wed.

Young Woman   Lie down. I'll be quick.

He crosses to the bed. She dips her fingers in the water, starts rubbing. **William** *whistles as he undresses and gets on the bed. A laughing vision of* **Gilbert** *now appears, wearing a dazzling white miller's apron. At his feet a sack of flour.*

William   You coming, woman?

Young Woman   I'm there, William, I'm . . .

She closes her eyes trying to get rid of him. Concurrent sound of rubbing hands, **William***'s whistling,* **Gilbert***'s just-audible laughter.*

How's the mare, William?

William   She's better . . .

Young Woman   O Sweet God in Heaven. . .

William   You saying, woman?

Gilbert *vanishes.*

Young Woman   Prayer before bed, William.

William   Best you do. Once you're down here, God can't help.

Snorts at his prurient wit. Fingers clean, she goes to the bed.

Scene Eleven

Same.

Darkness before dawn. **Gilbert**'s *vision has reappeared. Takes flour from sack, claps hands. Great flour-clouds in the air.* **Young Woman** *in a loose shift moves in her sleep, sneezes and wakes.*

Young Woman   ...! Out this house! You! Out! William, run him out. William.

Turns to wake **William**: *bed's empty.*

What you done with him...? I'll fetch him in. He'll rid you! He'll finish you!

Runs out to the stables. Approaches door, pauses, listens, raises her hand to knock. Before she can, **William**'s *voice is heard.*

William   'S it, sweet. You're a lovely one. A good one.

Young Woman *softens, shoulders drop. Smiles with joy, relief.*

Young Woman   Sweet God in Heaven, the foal's come. Oh. Thank you.

Again **William**'s *soft, warm voice. She listens, enjoying it.*

William   Take your time ... good and slow ... you're a lovely one, a lovely one. O, my sweet.

From within comes female laughter. **Young Woman** *stares at the stable doors. The laugh again. She runs into the house, looking for*

Gilbert. *Goes to her clothes, then out the house and off.*

Scene Twelve

Countryside.

Before dawn.

Young Woman   When the sun comes back the warm wind will blow on my face. When I look up I will see the sun shine bright in the sky. The clouds will ... be white. The crops ... the strong crops will grow on the good field. The bird will sing on the tall tree. The tall tree will ... stand and the warm wind will shake the leaves. The rabbit will run on the good field where the strong crops grow. New day will start and end the night. Night will be gone.

Scene Thirteen

Gilbert*'s house.*

Young Woman   Bastard! Open up! Take it off!

Gilbert   ... Ploughman, you there? I never touched her. Never would. Know she's yours.

Young Woman   You know where he's, miller. You charmed him. Only me here. Only me here, filth. Open your door. Stand here till you do, boy. (*Door opens.*) You take it off us, miller! You take it off!

Gilbert   What you wanting?

Young Woman   Take your charm off me and my ploughman. What we done?

Gilbert   You're talking madness.

Young Woman   You got envy of us! See it now. In the eyes.

Gilbert   Go home.

Young Woman I'll get other men out here. You do it with this, ih? Tricker. Water washed it off. Can't be a strong charm. Got in my head. Climbed in. Laughing. Throwing flour over us. 'S your magic. Charming him out to the stables. Making your laugh a woman's. That it gone now?

She's torn the paper as she spoke.

Gilbert A woman's laugh?

Young Woman That it gone? Tell me, miller.

Gilbert D'you look in the stables, horse-wife?

Young Woman Wasn't looking at any more'f your tricks.

Gilbert A woman's laugh. Ha ha.

Young Woman Take it off, miller . . . Please. Beg you. You want to lie with me? That it. Leave us then. Here. Pleasure for you under here, miller.

Gilbert Get up . . . All I need's to kiss you.

She goes to kiss him. He gets lost in it, in her.

Young Woman Gone now, oh . . . 'S it off, miller, ih? (*He shrugs.*) What's that? 'S gone now.

Gilbert Dunno. Just wanted to kiss you. Only charm I know.

As he grins, he's violently punched by **Young Woman**, *falls.*

Young Woman O God make this man die in cold pain! Evil!

Gilbert FUCK OFF YOU! I got no magic! FUCK OFF AWAY FROM ME! Fuck off back to your silent village! Fuck off back to your greedy man! 'N run! RUN!! You'll catch the Robertson girl still licking on his tired cock.

Young Woman *has backed away. He slams the door. She stands still, alone outside his house.*

Scene Fourteen

Gilbert's *house.*

Much later. **Young Woman** *still outside.* **Gilbert** *comes to put a blanket around her. She turns and walks into the house, sits at the table, picks up the pen, begins writing on the sheets of paper there.*

Scene Fifteen

Inside **Gilbert**'s *house.*

Young Woman *wakes from sleep at the table, aware of his blanket around her.*

Gilbert   'S evening. Better'n any bed, that soft paper. Lay down on it myself.

Young Woman   Why'm I here? What you done to me?

Gilbert   Nothing. You held the pen yourself.

Young Woman *looks at the pen, sees the paper, reads.*

Young Woman   'This is me. I live now. Others have, more will. I was born here because God wanted it. He had me sit in my mother till I could look at all that is his world. Every thing I see and know is put in my head by God. Every thing he created is there every day, sunrise to sundown, earth to sky. It cannot be touched or held the way I touch a table or hold the reins of a horse. It cannot be sold or cooked. His world is there, in front of my eyes. All I must do is push names into what is there the same as when I push my knife into the stomach of a hen. This is how I know God is there. I look at a tree and say tree then walk on. But there is more of the tree that is God which I have no names for. Each day I want to know more. A puddle I can see under. A tree when it is blown by the wind. A carrot that is sweeter than the others. The cold earth under a rock. The warm breath of a tired horse.

A man's face in the evening after work. The sound a woman makes when no one hears her. I know now I must find out the names for myself. I must stand and look close at every thing and God will reward me. This is how I will know God better. The village has lied. William has lied. It is not because I am undeserving. Not because I am young and they are old. God has given them nothing. I know this now. I see William ploughing a field. I have no name for the thing which is in my head. It is not envy. It is more than envy. It does not scare me. I must look close enough to discover what it is. Every thing in my head is put there by God. Every name I have will take me closer to him.

She picks up the pen and begins writing again.

'S not envy. No. What is it? What is it? What's this thing? William. (*Finishes writing.*) Tell me 's not you done this.

Gilbert   No.

Young Woman   I've no torment or misery. Then it is God. It is God.

She sheds the blanket, walks to the door, looks at him, goes out. He stares at what she's written.

Scene Sixteen

Cottage. Night.

William *in bed.* **Young Woman** *standing above him.*

William   ... 'S that? You? ... Woman ...?

Young Woman   Yes, William.

William   Haw ... Where you been?

Young Woman   The last field.

William   Hh?

Young Woman   The furthest over. Said I'd walk out to it one day. Come back and tell you what I seen.

William   You been gone the full day, woman . . .

Young Woman   I was praying.

William   For a full day?

Young Woman   For us, William. Praying for us and what we have. Was so beautiful I had to pray, William. Longer God's given the greater his reward. Asked for a full harvest, William.

William   'S good.

Young Woman   'N the horses to stand strong.

William   'S the right prayer.

Young Woman   'N the mare. Prayed for her.

William   Her foal'll be here by the week's end.

Young Woman   Don't want her hurting more. Or moaning. Like she does.

William   You tell me'f you go out there again.

Young Woman   I will.

William   You live here, you stay here. No going off and saying nothing.

He goes to her, arms around her.

'S good to feel you, woman. Whole village I searched for you. 'You seen my woman?' 'You seen my woman?'

Young Woman   What'd they say?

William   None had.

Young Woman   How far'd you come out the village, William?

William   Couldn't go far. I had a field to plough. And the new mill-stone pulled upright ready for rolling tomorrow.

Young Woman Tomorrow?

William 'S why I needed you back. 'S our first 'rolling-of-the-stone' as man and wife. Us men need you women to shout us on. Now come to bed, woman.

Young Woman I had to go, William. Had to see this field. You were right. It is like me. 'S a beautiful field.

William 'S what I said. Now come down, woman, come down.

Young Woman You need washing 'fore sleep, William?

William No.

Young Woman You done it?

William No wife here to help. Not take roughness and sweat on you for a night?

Later in the night.

Gilbert *has appeared again.* **Young Woman** *moves pleasurably on the bed, eyes open. She crosses to take flour from the sack, rubs it on herself.* **William** *screams in his sleep.*

William Uuaaaghhh! Uh . . . oh.

Gilbert *disappears. She returns to the bed.*

Young Woman William.

William Oh . . . You not hear it, woman? 'S falling off you. Oh.

Young Woman What?

William Skin . . . your skin . . . I'd my hands on you, touching and it came off . . . like cattle hide. Dry. Oh. Tore off warm. Left you with holes all over, and . . . your eyes never opened. You not hear it, woman? Tearing. Oh. You not hear it? Oh. Needing water.

He stumbles away. She lies down.

Scene Seventeen

Village. Outside the stonemason's.

Noise of villagers. **William** *and* **Young Woman**.

William   Look at the rock! Look at its size. Stonemason!
You've made your village proud. 'S the finest stone ever
been carved. Best time of year, this. All the village together.
God knows. Given us the day for it. Shining sun and the
west wind. 'S what we asked for. Hold yourself, miller,
sitting alone in your mill. When the stone rolls, the earth
thunders! Be sure and keep up, woman. Shout your
stoneman on.

Scene Eighteen

Outside mill.

Young Woman *and* **William** *sit after the new mill-stone's been
placed.* **Gilbert** *comes on carrying a whisky keg.*

William   What you want, miller? We rest now.

Gilbert   To thank the village for its labour and its sweat.

William   We roll the stone for us, miller. Our rent can
only be paid with flour.

Young Woman   And our bread only baked with it.

Gilbert   Will you've a miller's dram of gratitude?

William   Have others drunk it?

Gilbert   Some have, some haven't.

William   I'll try your potion, miller.

Young Woman   William, make him drink it first.

Gilbert *drinks, proffers it to* **William**.

Gilbert   She's a beautiful stone ... more than stone –
monument. A second church. Carved from love and life in
equal parts.

Young Woman   'N who takes it? The most undeserving.

William *laughs*.

Gilbert   Will your woman take a drop?

William   Will you, woman?

Young Woman   I will. 'S water, not whisky! Weak and cold.

William   Woman's right.

Young Woman   You wash in it, miller? That how you brew it?

Gilbert   Does me. Out here.

Young Woman   No one to help drink it, 's why.

William   I'll have more. Rid you of it.

Young Woman   You want good whisky, miller, come to the village. Buy from us.

William   Off now, miller. Leave us.

Young Woman *slumps to the ground*.

William   Woman . . . ? Woman! What you done, miller?!

Gilbert   . . . I done nothing.

William   This's you, I'll kill you.

Gilbert   Swear, ploughman.

William   Woman . . . (*Feels her face.*) Stupid woman. Stupid. Standing on a field for a day. Too many prayers and no food. We've work to finish. Not wanting to see the old stone broken up?

Gilbert   Ploughman. I want it kept.

William   No. 'S old. Finished. This's work the men want.

Gilbert   'M asking you, ploughman. I want it kept. Was

the last stone turned by me and my wife. Served me well.
Served the village well.

William   Where you want it, miller? Rolled to your bed?

Gilbert   Behind the house's a shed. Stand it along the far
wall.

William   Nnh.

Gilbert   'S a long walk home. I've a fire built inside.
Your woman'd be better by its warmth.

William   'F you can, take her in. 'S work you know,
miller. Carrying women.

Gilbert   My thanks again, ploughman.

William   Been told. Don't want your thanks. You be
standing when I'm back, woman.

William *goes.* **Gilbert** *shouts to him.*

Gilbert   Ploughman! Tell your men to cover the face.
Shed's my privy.

Turns to see **Young Woman** *sitting up. They both walk off.*

Scene Nineteen

Gilbert's *house.*

Young Woman *on the bed.* **Gilbert** *by her.* **William** *comes
in.*

William   Woman? On your feet. Village's gone. Woman.
You got nothing for her, miller? Give you money.

Gilbert   I've nothing.

William   'S night, woman. I need sleep. No horse have
you, miller?

Gilbert   No need of one. Sleep here with her.

William   Can't sleep on any bed but my own.

Gilbert   Carry her yourself.

William   After two mill-stones and your whisky? (*Looks around.*) 'S where you sit your nights?

Gilbert   Front've a fire like you.

William   'N do what?

Gilbert   Cook. Smoke. Read.

William   Why d'you have all them books?

Gilbert   So's when I finish one I can read another.

William   That why you got them standing up like that, touching? Don't look right. Nothing else here. Must feel the need of more, eh?

Gilbert   More of what?

William *indicates the* **Young Woman**.

. . . I'm a man like you.

William   You're a miller, miller. Not like me. Nothing like me.

Gilbert   'S only a special woman wants to know a miller. Most believe we've dead worms in our trousers.

William   More'n that, miller. More'n what's in the trousers. More hate'n that. Where you been?

Gilbert   Doesn't trouble me now, ploughman.

William   You must pray to be one of us, miller. The country over you're hated. Even the children run from you. Ever ask why that is? You get part of our grain for milling it. That's law. But we hate you more'n that law. We're stupid and cruel. Blind. Hate you more'n any thing I can name. Why's that, miller? Why's it like that? Your wife was a miller's daughter, wasn't she? Had to be. 'D she love you? . . . 'D you love her? How long since you seen a woman here, miller? Lying on her back. What you got in your head, looking at her? Look at her. Look. A new country. D'you remember the colours of it, how fallow it looks, how it takes your breath? Fresh earth. Mist. Grass around rock. D'you remember the smell? D'you remember the strength? How you believe you're destroying her with your shape, making a new land, God that you are. D'you remember how she turns? How she loses you? Legs. Neck. Stomach. Arms. Breast. Wrong names they are, miller. Who named them? Never the same's men's. Never. Women've no legs. No arms. They've more. I got names for them. My own names. She knows. No one else.

Gilbert   Loved my wife.

William (*laughs*)   Village'd run me out for that talk.

Gilbert   Why?

William   You stand in church, same's me.

Gilbert   Never listen.

William   'The glory of God is God, not his creation.' 'S what they say now. I need to piss. You believe that, miller? Glory of God's God, not his creation.

Gilbert   Dunno.

William   'S that not God there? You look. 'S that not? You gone without too long. You look at it. You remember.

Gilbert   She's your wife.

William   I'm a ploughman, miller. Earth gets weak you keep turning it. You got to rest it. Always other fields to start on. – More God.

Gilbert   You know where's the shed. Walk to the sound of the river.

William   Fool you believe I'm going in this blackness.

He takes a candle, goes out. **Young Woman** *sits up, walks to the door, goes out.* **Gilbert** *follows.*

Scene Twenty

Shed.

William *using the privy. The old mill-stone in candlelight.* **Young Woman** *and* **Gilbert** *emerge from behind it. They push the stone over.*

Scene Twenty-One

Gilbert*'s house.*

Gilbert *and* **Young Woman** *opposite each other, watching the other slowly undress. From the shed come* **William***'s faint death screams. The screams fade. They walk to the bed.*

Scene Twenty-Two

Gilbert*'s house.*

After. **Young Woman** *and* **Gilbert** *lying together.*

Young Woman   You've said nothing.

Gilbert   Waiting for him to stop.

Young Woman   Who? Pony William? Village ploughman? Listen. He's gone. You can talk now.

Gilbert   Tell me what's in your head?

Young Woman   You. Filth. Evil-breath. Bastard miller. Why?

Gilbert   I got some thing in here, some thing –

Young Woman   What?

Pause.

Look. Sun's rising.

Gilbert   Same's yesterday.

Young Woman   Never seen it from the mill. Never seen these colours. 'S the thing in your head. Look. 'S God giving us more'f what He is. Look. New world front'f us. The morning I ran here, you said, you shouted – ... Fuck ... Off.

Gilbert   Fuck off.

Young Woman   No one's ever said that to me. Never heard it before.

Gilbert   First time I've ever said it.

Young Woman   'S it mean?

Gilbert   Dunno. Was shouted at market. A Bible-seller back from Germany. A boy was pissing against his stall.

Young Woman   Fuck. Off. 'S mine now.

Gilbert   Before, standing there ... he said, your ploughman said – 'What you got in your head, miller, looking at her?' You hear him? I saw my wife. Woman that was my wife. Then you were there. In here. My head. No clothes. Pushing. Sweating. Groaning like the wind. Eyes open, arms open, I was in your mouth, at your cunt, in your hair. 'S it God put you there? My body was like nothing I've known in my life. 'S it God did that? No ... Not God. Was what your ploughman said. Was his words.

Young Woman   No.

Gilbert   His words made me do that.

Young Woman   All his talk's lies.

Gilbert   In my own head. Was me.

Young Woman   No. Ploughman couldn't see. He knew nothing. I'm not like any thing. You seen that.

Gilbert   Was me.

Young Woman   You seen that. Tell me you seen that now.

Gilbert   Not God. Me. You not understand, woman?

Young Woman   No.

Gilbert   In my own head.

Young Woman   Stop this talk. 'S him. 'S him.

Gilbert   Where you going?

Young Woman   Ploughman needs buried. His mouth filled up with earth.

Gilbert   Bury him here?

Young Woman   'S near full light. I've to walk back to the village.

Gilbert   'Cos'f what I said. About your God.

Young Woman   No. I've to tell them. William's gone. Bed's empty and cold. Fields empty. Stables empty.

Gilbert   They'll still come for me – your village.

Young Woman   The hated miller.

Gilbert   Can't live without their ploughman.

Young Woman   No. 'He's left me. He's gone for a better wife. He walked away in the night. I sit alone by the fire. Look at my tear puddles. I'm the broken-hearted wife.'

Gilbert   How long?

Young Woman   Until what? Until they believe.

Gilbert   And after?

Young Woman   Live in the mill?

Gilbert   Live in the village?

She goes.

'S not You. 'S me.

Scene Twenty-Three

Stables.

Young Woman *delivers the mare's pony.*

Young Woman   Sshh ... Don't get scared. Feel my hands. Warm hands. Wife of William. Friend. Strong. Quiet. There. Breathe now. Sshh ... Here it comes. Push, love, push. Head and neck. Eyes. Push a last time. Sssh ... There. There. Look, mother ... Life. A new horse in the world.

Scene Twenty-Four

Field. Day.

Some time after. **Young Woman** *stands looking around her. Mouths silently to herself.* **Gilbert** *appears.*

Gilbert   Day's over. You not walk back with the rest of the village? They say you speak to no one. Heard them talk about you at my mill. Works in the fields. Cares for the horses. Sits in her house at night. Not one word.

Young Woman   Why speak to any of them? Village believed me.

Gilbert   Broken-hearted wife.

Young Woman   Said all I needed to.

Gilbert   They never came for me.

Young Woman   You never ran.

Gilbert   Village'll find an empty mill tomorrow.

Young Woman   Where's the miller gone?

Gilbert   To the town won't call me 'miller'.

Young Woman   Have to walk far.

Gilbert   See more'f the world. Seen all this. Know all

this. Nothing left for me. Every thing I have 's in here.

Young Woman   Things change every time I look at them. Each has a name.

Gilbert   Still see you. Every day I wake. Still hear his words.

Young Woman   So many names. I'll learn every one.

Gilbert   I want more. In the town there's books and pens and paper. Owned by people who've left villages. They speak all day about every thing in the world.

Young Woman   'S what you been told?

Gilbert   Have to believe some thing.

Young Woman   New things in my head. Every time I look. New names. Don't need somewhere else.

Gilbert   There's more the village's saying.

Young Woman   What?

Gilbert   Was you pulled the new horse out alone.

Young Woman   Horses trust me now.

Gilbert   You looked at it close?

Young Woman   'S a beautiful horse. Quick and strong.

Gilbert   Village's saying it's William. Say's Pony William running on the field.

Young Woman   Say more'n that. Say he's happier now than he ever was. Village's right. Pony is.

Gilbert   Here, horse-wife. Write what you know now. Write what you see.

He has given her the pen. He leaves.

Young Woman   Village needs a new miller.

End.

Methuen Contemporary Dramatists
include

John Arden (two volumes)
Arden & D'Arcy
Peter Barnes (three volumes)
Sebastian Barry
Dermot Bolger
Edward Bond (six volumes)
Howard Brenton
  (two volumes)
Richard Cameron
Jim Cartwright
Caryl Churchill (two volumes)
Sarah Daniels (two volumes)
Nick Darke
David Edgar (three volumes)
Ben Elton
Dario Fo (two volumes)
Michael Frayn (three volumes)
David Greig
John Godber (two volumes)
Paul Godfrey
John Guare
Lee Hall (two volumes)
Peter Handke
Jonathan Harvey
  (two volumes)
Declan Hughes
Terry Johnson (two volumes)
Sarah Kane
Barrie Keefe
Bernard-Marie Koltès
David Lan
Bryony Lavery
Deborah Levy
Doug Lucie

David Mamet (four volumes)
Martin McDonagh
Duncan McLean
Anthony Minghella
  (two volumes)
Tom Murphy (four volumes)
Phyllis Nagy
Anthony Neilsen
Philip Osment
Louise Page
Stewart Parker (two volumes)
Joe Penhall
Stephen Poliakoff
  (three volumes)
David Rabe
Mark Ravenhill
Christina Reid
Philip Ridley
Willy Russell
Eric-Emmanuel Schmitt
Ntozake Shange
Sam Shepard (two volumes)
Shelagh Stephenson
Wole Soyinka (two volumes)
David Storey (three volumes)
Sue Townsend
Judy Upton
Michel Vinaver
  (two volumes)
Arnold Wesker (two volumes)
Michael Wilcox
Roy Williams
Snoo Wilson (two volumes)
David Wood (two volumes)
Victoria Wood

Methuen Student Editions

Jean Anouilh	*Antigone*
John Arden	*Serjeant Musgrave's Dance*
Alan Ayckbourn	*Confusions*
Aphra Behn	*The Rover*
Edward Bond	*Lear*
Bertolt Brecht	*The Caucasian Chalk Circle*
	Life of Galileo
	Mother Courage and her Children
	The Resistible Rise of Arturo Ui
	The Threepenny Opera
Anton Chekhov	*The Cherry Orchard*
	The Seagull
	Three Sisters
	Uncle Vanya
Caryl Churchill	*Serious Money*
	Top Girls
Shelagh Delaney	*A Taste of Honey*
Euripides	*Medea*
	Elektra
Dario Fo	*Accidental Death of an Anarchist*
Michael Frayn	*Copenhagen*
John Galsworthy	*Strife*
Nikolai Gogol	*The Government Inspector*
Robert Holman	*Across Oka*
Henrik Ibsen	*A Doll's House*
	Hedda Gabler
Charlotte Keatley	*My Mother Said I Never Should*
Bernard Kops	*Dreams of Anne Frank*
Federico García Lorca	*Blood Wedding*
	The House of Bernarda Alba
	(bilingual edition)
David Mamet	*Glengarry Glen Ross*
	Oleanna
Luigi Pirandello	*Six Characters in Search of an Author*
Mark Ravenhill	*Shopping and F***ing*
Willy Russell	*Blood Brothers*
Wole Soyinka	*Death and the King's Horseman*
J. M. Synge	*The Playboy of the Western World*
Oscar Wilde	*The Importance of Being Earnest*
Tennessee Williams	*A Streetcar Named Desire*
	The Glass Menagerie
Timberlake Wertenbaker	*Our Country's Good*

Methuen Modern Plays

include work by

Edward Albee
Jean Anouilh
John Arden
Margaretta D'Arcy
Peter Barnes
Sebastian Barry
Brendan Behan
Dermot Bolger
Edward Bond
Bertolt Brecht
Howard Brenton
Anthony Burgess
Simon Burke
Jim Cartwright
Caryl Churchill
Noël Coward
Lucinda Coxon
Sarah Daniels
Nick Darke
Nick Dear
Shelagh Delaney
David Edgar
David Eldridge
Dario Fo
Michael Frayn
John Godber
Paul Godfrey
David Greig
John Guare
Peter Handke
David Harrower
Jonathan Harvey
Iain Heggie
Declan Hughes
Terry Johnson
Sarah Kane
Charlotte Keatley
Barrie Keeffe
Howard Korder

Robert Lepage
Doug Lucie
Martin McDonagh
John McGrath
Terrence McNally
David Mamet
Patrick Marber
Arthur Miller
Mtwa, Ngema & Simon
Tom Murphy
Phyllis Nagy
Peter Nichols
Sean O'Brien
Joseph O'Connor
Joe Orton
Louise Page
Joe Penhall
Luigi Pirandello
Stephen Poliakoff
Franca Rame
Mark Ravenhill
Philip Ridley
Reginald Rose
Willy Russell
Jean-Paul Sartre
Sam Shepard
Wole Soyinka
Shelagh Stephenson
Peter Straughan
C. P. Taylor
Theatre de Complicite
Theatre Workshop
Sue Townsend
Judy Upton
Timberlake Wertenbaker
Roy Williams
Snoo Wilson
Victoria Wood

Methuen World Classics
include

Jean Anouilh (two volumes)
Brendan Behan
Aphra Behn
Bertolt Brecht (eight volumes)
Büchner
Bulgakov
Calderón
Čapek
Anton Chekhov
Noël Coward (eight volumes)
Feydeau
Eduardo De Filippo
Max Frisch
John Galsworthy
Gogol
Gorky (two volumes)
Harley Granville Barker
    (two volumes)
Victor Hugo
Henrik Ibsen (six volumes)
Jarry

Lorca (three volumes)
Marivaux
Mustapha Matura
David Mercer (two volumes)
Arthur Miller (five volumes)
Molière
Musset
Peter Nichols (two volumes)
Joe Orton
A. W. Pinero
Luigi Pirandello
Terence Rattigan
    (two volumes)
W. Somerset Maugham
    (two volumes)
August Strindberg
    (three volumes)
J. M. Synge
Ramón del Valle-Inclán
Frank Wedekind
Oscar Wilde